A To Z Creatures Of The Amazon

I0622158

Elizabeth Van Nguyen

Dedication

To my mother and father, thank you for everything!

Acknowledgment

Thank you to all the people who helped make this book a reality!

It's been a delightful experience!

Page Blank Intentionally

A is for the Amazonian Royal Flycatcher. The Amazonian Royal Flycatcher is a spectacle to see, especially their nests, which can be more than six feet long. They perch on branches over water, quite safe from predators that want a snack to snatch. [1,2]

This photograph has been taken from Shutter Stock.

B is for Blue Morpho Butterfly. The Blue Morpho Butterfly can be seen from far above. Its beautiful blue wings flutter all about, but when straight and still, it spans approximately eight inches across! Surprisingly, they don't feed on nectar like most butterflies but instead sip on juices for their short two-week adult lifespan.[3]

This photograph has been taken from Freepik.

C is for Greater Capybara. The Greater Capybara is the largest rodent worldwide. No other relative even comes close in size! This biggest rodent in the world eats its own excrement to help digest the grass it grazes on. Additionally, it swims with webbed feet and can stay underwater for up to five minutes.[5]

This photograph has been taken from Freepik.

D is for the Amazon River Dolphin. Sadly, this fascinating creature is endangered. It is the only freshwater river dolphin that lives in the Amazon River. Amazon River Dolphin relies on a special skill called echolocation for hunting prey like fish, turtles, and crabs. Even though they are nearly blind, Amazon River Dolphins come in a range of colors, from pink to gray! [6,7]

This photograph has been taken from Shutter Stock.

E is for Great Egret. The Great Egret is snowy white from head to toe. They can be found in many places around the world. They like catching fish, frogs, and even slippery snakes for dinner. During mating season, Great Egrets get all dressed up! Like a peacock, they grow long, feathery plumes around their head and neck. These feathers help them attract a mate to start a family. [8,9]

This photograph has been taken from Freepik.

F is for Fire Ant. These tiny red ants have a powerful sting, so it's best to admire them from a distance. Their colonies can take months to find, and they mine tunnels up to twenty feet deep. Be careful with your tropical fruit, as these ants have spread beyond their native habitat through cargo shipments. So next time you have a yummy banana, watch for an aggressive Fire ant that might be waiting to defend itself! [10,11]

This photograph has been taken from Shutter Stock.

G is for Giant Otter. The giant otter is the largest otter in the world. These animals love to munch on fish and live in dens along the banks of the Amazon River. They are super social and live in groups of up to twenty otters. Giant Otters are great at keeping their home safe and work together to chase away intruders.[12]

This photograph has been taken from Shutter Stock.

H is for Harpy Eagle. The Harpy Eagle is the largest and most powerful eagle in the Americas. With talons measuring four to five inches long, they have the most enormous talons of any living eagle. Harpy Eagles can lift prey that weigh as much as they do, including opossums, sloths, and monkeys.[13,14]

This photograph has been taken from Shutter Stock.

is for Green Thornytail Iguana. The Green Thornytail Iguana isn't often seen in the Amazon Rainforest because it dwells in the treetops. This small iguana grows up to three and a half inches long and primarily feeds on ants.[15]

This photograph has been taken from Shutter Stock.

J is for Jaguar. The Jaguar is the largest big cat in South America. Jaguars are usually solitary animals, and each Jaguar has unique spots. They are active during the day as well as at night and are comfortable in trees, on land, and in water. Their hunting keeps other animal populations in check. Jaguars mark their territory with their feces and paw engravings on trees. Their only predator and threat are humans.[16]

This photograph has been taken from Freepik.

K is for Kinkajou. The Kinkajou ("KIN" + "kuh" + "joo") is a nocturnal animal that loves sweet foods. These treetop dwellers are omnivores, although they mostly consume fruit. Their tail acts like an extra hand as it can grasp tree branches, and their paws can rotate backward! Despite their cute appearance, kinkajous do not make good pets because they carry parasites that are harmful to humans.[18]

This photograph has been taken from Shutter Stock.

L is for Green Basilisk Lizard. Surprisingly, this lizard can zip across water on its back legs! They're always close to a pond or river, which is their primary escape. Green Basilisk Lizards mostly munch on berries and insects and can grow up to two feet long![19]

This photograph has been taken from Shutter Stock.

M is for Amazon Rainforest Scarlet Macaw. The Amazon Rainforest Scarlet Macaw is an endangered species due to the pet trade and habitat loss. These brightly colored birds live primarily in the tallest trees of the rainforest canopy, where they can live for up to eighty years! [20]

This photograph has been taken from Freepik.

N is for Northern Night Monkey. The northern night monkey is a nocturnal species also known as the three-striped night monkey or the northern owl monkey. These monkeys are omnivores and live in family groups. They find a mate for life, or until that mate dies, and once the babies grow up, the offspring of the parents break ties.[21]

This photograph has been taken from Shutter Stock.

O is for Ocelot. The Ocelot is a cat with a coat that helps it camouflage, especially during the day when they are sleeping. They are up and about at night searching for meals like rabbits, rodents, iguanas, fish, frogs, monkeys, and birds. Ocelots have to watch out for bigger predators as they are food for anacondas, harpy eagles, jaguars, and pumas. Ocelots have a special way of eating – they rip their food into bite-sized pieces without needing to chew! [22]

This photograph has been taken from Freepik.

P is for Poison Dart Frog. These amphibians are about one inch long. Its bright color serves as a warning to other animals that it's toxic. In fact, it's considered the most venomous animal in the world. The "dart" part of its name originates from indigenous people using their poison on darts. Although it is not confirmed officially, it's believed that poison dart frogs acquire their toxicity from their diet..[23,24]

This photograph has been taken from Shutter Stock.

Q is for Pavonine Quetzal. The Pavonine Quetzal inhabits the lower canopy level. This bird has brightly colored feathers and a red bill for the males. They don't travel long distances during flight. Their unique toe arrangement makes it difficult for them to move on the ground.[25]

This photograph has been taken from Shutter Stock.

R is for Red Howler Monkey. The Red Howler Monkey is the largest among howler monkeys. They prefer to stay high up in trees, where they can easily find leaves to eat. The bottom third of their tails lacks fur, which helps them grip branches as they climb. Male monkeys typically lead a group of females and their offspring. In the mornings and evenings, red male howler monkeys howl to communicate with other groups and establish territorial boundaries. Their howls can be heard up to two miles away. [26]

This photograph has been taken from Shutter Stock.

S is for Scorpion. Scorpions give birth to live young, which ride on their mother's back until they molt. An outstanding trait they possess is the ability to survive without food for a year. Scorpions glow blue under ultraviolet light, even in fossils! They are nocturnal creatures that will consume almost anything they encounter. While they produce venom, scorpions generally pose little harm to humans.[27]

This photograph has been taken from Freepik.

T is for White-Throated Toucan. The White-Throated Toucan is the second largest toucan species. It's known for its bright colors and large bill, which it mainly uses to eat fruits. Although it is not the most skilled flier, it often lives with another toucan of the same species or in a group. [28]

This photograph has been taken from Shutter Stock.

U is for Bald Uakari. Bald uakaris have bright red faces when they are healthy. The redder the face, the more likely the monkey will find a mate. Bald uakaris with pale faces are considered unhealthy. These monkeys are very social and live with their family or friends in groups of up to thirty! They sleep high up in the canopy of the trees and keep close to the Amazon River. This is a great spot for two reasons – they can find food of their choice during the day, and they're safe from the rising river waters when the river overflows.[29]

This photograph has been taken from Shutter Stock.

V is for King Vulture. The King Vulture is the largest vulture in the New World. It's a scavenger and typically a solitary animal, although they form family units. This colorful bird usually mates for life and is rarely seen because it stays high up in the canopy or soars high above the ground in search of food.[30]

This photograph has been taken from Freepik.

W is for Brazilian Wandering Spider. The Brazilian wandering spider is the most venomous spider in the world. They have a lifespan of one to two years and don't construct webs. Their hairy bodies reach up to two inches, and their legs span up to seven inches. At night, they roam the rainforest floor in search of food.[31]

This photograph has been taken from Shutter Stock.

X is for Slender-billed Xenops. The slender-billed Xenops is a small, brown bird found in the rainforest canopy. It is not seen often and is known to join mixed-species flocks. It uses its skills to investigate dead brush in search of food.[32]

This photograph has been taken from Yandex.

Y is for the Yellow-spotted Amazon River Turtle. The Yellow-spotted Amazon River Turtle is most active during mid-morning and afternoon. Females of this species grow larger than males. While yellow-spotting is visible on young turtles and adult males, females lose their yellow-spotting altogether as they mature. These turtles can survive up to seventy years in the wild.[33]

This photograph has been taken from Freepik.

Z is for Zamurito. The Zamurito is a catfish that can reach up to sixteen inches in length. They are known for attacking other fish caught by fishermen. This species is also known by other names such as Vulture Catfish and Piracatinga.[34,35]

This photograph has been taken from Yandex.

Notes

1. Walker, Niccoy. "Amazonian Royal Flycatcher." a-z-animals.com. A-Z Animals, November 15, 2022. https://a-z-animals.com/animals/amazonian-royal-flycatcher/.

2. Atkins, Don. "What Is the Amazonian Royal Flycatcher Nest?" savetheeaglesinternational.org. SAVE THE EAGLES, April 16, 2024. https://savetheeaglesinternational.org/what-is-the-amazonian-royal-flycatcher-nest/.

3. "Blue Morpho Butterfly." Amazon Aid. Amazon Aid Foundation. Accessed May 13, 2024. https://amazonaid.org/species/blue-morpho-butterfly/.

4. Suzanne. "Life Cycle of the Blue Morpho Butterfly | Butterfly Lady." Butterfly Lady, August 19, 2018. http://butterfly-lady.com/life-cycle-of-the-blue-morpho-butterfly/.

5. "13 Surprising Capybara Facts." Fact Animal. Accessed May 13, 2024. https://factanimal.com/capybara/.

6. "Amazon River Dolphin." OneKindPlanet. OneKind, 2016. https://www.onekindplanet.org/animal/amazon-river-dolphin/.

7. "Pink Dolphins: Your Guide to the Amazon River's Boto Dolphin." Xplore Our Planet. Accessed May 13, 2024. https://xploreourplanet.com/conservation/Pink-dolphins.

8. Gilman, Salma. "6 Fascinating Birds to Find on an Amazon River Expedition." www.expeditions.com, 2024. https://www.expeditions.com/expedition-stories/stories/fascinating-birds-to-find-on-an-ama zon-river-expedition.

9. "Great Egret." a-z-animals.com. A-Z-Animals, March 13, 2022. https://a-z-animals.com/animals/great-egret/.

10. "Fire Ants Uncovered: Behavior, Impact, and Control Strategies." StaySafe.org, August 8, 2023. https://staysafe.org/pest-control/fire-ants/.

11. "Fire Ant Facts." MISSISSIPPI STATE UNIVERSITY EXTENSION. Mississippi State University, 2020. https://extension.msstate.edu/content/fire-ant-facts.

12. Active Wild Admin. "Giant River Otter, Pteronura Brasiliensis, Giant Otter: Facts & Pictures." Active Wild, August 24, 2017. https://www.activewild.com/giant-otter-facts/.

13. Shaner, Kyle. "Harpia Harpyja (Harpy Eagle)." Animal Diversity Web, 2011. https://animaldiversity.org/accounts/Harpia_harpyja/.

14. "Harpy Eagle." ANIMALIA. Accessed May 14, 2024. https://animalia.bio/harpy-eagle.

15. "Uracentron Azureum." wikiwand. Accessed May 14, 2024. https://www.wikiwand.com/en/Uracentron_azureum.

16. Editorial Staff. "35 Interesting Facts about Jaguars." theFACTfile, October 17, 2022. https://thefactfile.org/jaguar-facts/.

17. "How to Pronounce Kinkajou in American English (1 out of 16)": youglish.com. Accessed May 14, 2024. https://youglish.com/pronounce/kinkajou/english/us.

18. "Kinkajou Facts." Fact Animal. Accessed May 14, 2024. https://factanimal.com/kinkajou/.

19. "Green Basilisk Lizard – Lizards That Can Walk on Water." Easy Science For KIDS, April 20, 2013. https://easyscienceforkids.com/all-about-the-green-basilisk-lizard/.

20. Spencer, Joanne. "Scarlet Macaw." Animal Corner. Accessed May 14, 2024.

https://animalcorner.org/animals/scarlet-macaw/.

21. "Northern Night Monkey (Aotus Trivirgatus)." iNaturalist. Accessed May 14, 2024. https://www.inaturalist.org/taxa/43413-Aotus-trivirgatus.

22. Shaw, Allyson. "Ocelot: Can You Spot It?" National Geographic Kids. National Geographic, April 2, 2015. https://kids.nationalgeographic.com/animals/mammals/facts/ocelot.

23. Oldham, Cydni. "Poison Dart Frog." Animals Network, August 17, 2018. https://animals.net/poison-dart-frog/.

24. "Jumping Marvels of the Amazon." wwf.panda.org. Accessed May 14, 2024. https://wwf.panda.org/discover/knowledge_hub/where_we_work/amazon/about_the_amazo n/wildlife_amazon/amphibians/.

25. "Pavonine Quetzal (Pharomachrus Pavoninus)." iNaturalist. Accessed May 14, 2024. https://www.inaturalist.org/taxa/20859-Pharomachrus-pavoninus.

26. "Red Howler Monkey." ANIMALIA. Accessed May 14, 2024. https://animalia.bio/red-howler-monkey#google_vignette.

27. Hadley, Debbie. "10 Fascinating Facts about Scorpions." ThoughtCo, 2019. https://www.thoughtco.com/scorpion-facts-4135393.

28. "WHITE-THROATED TOUCAN." ANIMALIA. Accessed May 14, 2024. https://animalia.bio/white-throated-toucan.

29. "Bald Uakari Facts." Fact Animal. Accessed May 14, 2024. https://factanimal.com/bald-uakari/.

30. "King Vulture." ANIMALIA. Accessed May 14, 2024. https://animalia.bio/king-vulture.

31. Szalay, Jessie , and Laura Geggel. "Brazilian Wandering Spiders: Bites & Other Facts." livescience.com. Live Science, December 19, 2021. https://www.livescience.com/41591-brazilian-wandering-spiders.html#Mating.

32. "Slender-Billed Xenops - Xenops Tenuirostris." ebird.org. eBird. Accessed May 14, 2024. https://ebird.org/species/slbxen1.

33. "Yellow-Spotted Amazon River Turtle." Smithsonian's National Zoo & Conservation Biology Institute. Smithsonian, April 25, 2016. https://nationalzoo.si.edu/animals/yellow-spotted-amazon-river-turtle.

34. "CALOPHYSUS MACROPTERUS." ANIMALIA. Accessed May 14, 2024. https://animalia.bio/calophysus-macropterus.

35. "Calophysus Macropterus – Zamurito." aquainfo.org. AQUAINFO. Accessed May 14, 2024. https://aquainfo.org/article/calophysus-macropterus-zamurito/.